CAIN
THE DESTROYER OF DREAMS

A STUDY OF THE FIRST RECORDED MURDER

JOHN MARINELLI

Cain
The Destroyer of Dreams
A Study of the First Recorded Murder
Copyright © 2023 John Marinelli
Ocala, Florida … All rights reserved.

First Edition: 7/2023

Print ISBN # 978-1-0881-6868-4
eBook ISBN # 978-1-0881-6874-5

Cover and Formatting: Streetlight Graphics
Contact: johnmarinelli@embarqmail.com

This book is protected under US copyright laws. Any reproduction or other use is prohibited without the written permission of the author.

No part of this book may be reproduced, scanned, or distributed in any printed or electronic form without permission. Please do not participate in or encourage piracy of copyrighted materials in violation of the author's rights. Thank you for respecting the hard work of this author.

TABLE OF CONTENTS

Preface 1

Introduction 3

The 1st Birth & The 1st Death on Earth 9

The Path of The Righteous 13

The Significance of The Story 17

The God-Man 19

The Seed of The Woman 23

The Sin Behind The Sin 27

Sin Lieth At The Door	31
The Cry of Innocent Blood	33
The Divine Replacement	37
The Seed of Promise	39
Cain, His Children & Their Legacy	41
The Origin of Polygamy	43
Enoch & Enoch	45
The Death of Cain & How He Died	47
The Mystery of Cain's Wife	49
The Gene Pool Question	51
The Mark Upon Cain	53
The Way of Cain	55
God's Judgment of Cain	57
Modern Day life Applications	59
Conclusion	63
About The Author John Marinelli	65

PREFACE

I had just about decided not to write anymore books. After all, I have over 20 books in print. I even told my proofreader and my wife that I would be taking a break and possibly not doing another book at all. Then I received an epiphany from the Lord. He gave me a very interesting title, "Cain, The Destroyer of Dreams."

The title was so unique that it just kept echoing in my mind. My curiosity pushed me to start asking questions. How did Cain destroy dreams? What was, "The Way of Cain?" Why did God place a mark on Cain? What kind of mark was it? Where did Cain's wife come from? How did Cain die? What legacy did the descendants of Cain enjoy? Why did Cain kill his brother, Abel? These questions and more had to be answered, so, I embarked on my journey to discover, and share all that I can find.

I looked first to the Bible where the story was first recorded. Then to ancient traditions and folklore. I even read various theories on the subject which some I will share as the content of my book unfolds.

I think that the most important lesson we can learn from this tragic story is how to guard our hearts against those things that led Cain to do what he did.

INTRODUCTION

The story of Cain and Abel is found in the Bible, specifically, the book of Genesis. It is a record of the 1st birth on earth and the 1st death. Oddly enough, the book, along with others was written by Moses, hundreds of years after it happened. It could have been floating through time in ancient tradition or it could have been a direct revelation from God to Moses.

It doesn't make any difference how it survived the centuries. The fact is, it did survive and ended up in the pages of the Bible. I figure that most of my readers will not actually sit down and read the story from Genesis so I will reprint it here in hopes that you will read it carefully. It's always important to check out the author's assumptions and statements before accepting them as fact.

Genesis Chapter Four

"And Adam knew Eve his wife; and she conceived, and bare Cain, and said, I have gotten a man from the LORD. And she again bare his brother Abel. And Abel was a keeper of sheep, but Cain was a tiller of the ground.

And in process of time, it came to pass, that Cain brought of the fruit of the ground an offering unto the LORD. And Abel, he also brought of the firstlings of his flock and of the fat thereof. And the LORD had respect unto Abel and to his offering:

But unto Cain and to his offering he had not respect. And Cain was very wroth, and his countenance fell. And the LORD said unto Cain, why art thou wroth? and why is thy countenance fallen? If thou doest well, shalt thou not be accepted? and if thou doest not well, sin lieth at the door. And unto thee shall be his desire, and thou shalt rule over him.

And Cain talked with Abel his brother: and it came to pass, when they were in the field, that Cain rose up against Abel his brother, and slew him. And the LORD said unto Cain, where is Abel thy brother? And he said, I know not: Am I my brother's keeper?

And he said, what hast thou done? the voice of thy brother's blood cries unto me from the ground. And now art thou cursed from the earth, which hath opened her mouth to receive thy brother's blood from thy hand; When thou till the ground, it shall not henceforth yield unto thee her strength; a fugitive and a vagabond shalt thou be in the earth. And Cain said unto the Lord, My punishment is greater than I can bear. Behold, thou hast driven me out this day from the face of the earth; and from thy face shall I be hid; and I shall be a fugitive and a vagabond in the earth; and it shall come to pass, that every one that finds me shall slay me.

And the Lord said unto him, Therefore, whosoever slays Cain, vengeance shall be taken on him sevenfold. And the Lord set a mark upon Cain, lest any finding him should kill him. And Cain went out from the presence of the Lord, and dwelt in the land of Nod, on the east of Eden.

And Cain knew his wife; and she conceived, and bare Enoch: and he built a city, and called the name of the city, after the name of his son, Enoch.

And unto Enoch was born Irad: and Irad begat Mehujael: and Mehujael begat Methusael: and Methusael begat Lamech. And Lamech took unto him two wives: the name of the one was Adah, and the name of the other Zillah.

And Adah bare Jabal: he was the father of such as dwell in tents, and of such as have cattle. And his brother's name was Jubal: he was the father of all, such as handle the harp and organ.

And Zillah, she also bare Tubalcain, an instructer of every artificer in brass and iron: and the sister of Tubalcain was Naamah.

And Lamech said unto his wives, Adah and Zillah, Hear my voice; ye wives of Lamech, hearken unto my speech: for I have slain a man to my wounding, and a young man to my hurt. If Cain shall be avenged sevenfold, truly Lamech seventy and sevenfold.

And Adam knew his wife again; and she bare a son, and called his name Seth: For God, said she, hath appointed me another seed instead of Abel, whom Cain slew. And to Seth, to him also there was born a son; and he called his name Enos: then began men to call upon the name of the LORD."

Interesting story, isn't it? Is it true or just a parable? Some say it is just a story and has no significance or roots in real facts. In other words, it cannot be verified in archeology. It's been over 6,000 years since it happened. I would think that coming from Moses would validate it as fact, wouldn't you? However, folks are allowed to be wrong. It just says to me that they do not want to discover the truth and benefit from its wisdom. Let's move on in our journey.

THE 1ST BIRTH & THE 1ST DEATH ON EARTH

Cain was the first human being to be born on earth. He came through the womb of Eve in child birth. What is it about Cain that we should know? Here's what Easton's Bible Dictionary says:

The first-born son of Adam and Eve (Genesis 4). He became a tiller of the ground, as his brother Abel followed the pursuits of pastoral life. He was "a sullen, self-willed, haughty, vindictive man; wanting the religious element in his character, and defiant even in his attitude towards God.

" It came to pass "in process of time" (marg. "at the end of days"), i.e., probably on the Sabbath, that the two brothers presented their offerings to the Lord. Abel's offering was of the "firstlings of his flock and of the fat," while Cain's was "of the fruit of the ground." Abel's sacrifice was "more excellent" (Hebrews 11:4) than Cain's, and was accepted by God.

On this account Cain was "very wroth," and cherished feelings of murderous hatred against his brother, and was at length guilty of the desperate outrage of putting him to death (1 John 3:12). For this crime he was expelled from Eden, and henceforth led the life of an exile, bearing upon him some mark which God had set upon him in answer to his own cry for mercy, so that thereby he might be protected from the wrath of his fellow-men; or it may be that God only gave him some sign to assure him that he would not be slain (Genesis 4:15).

Doomed to be a wanderer and a fugitive in the earth, he went forth into the "land of Nod", i.e., the land of "exile", which is said to have been in the "east of Eden," and there he built a city, the first we read of, and called it after his son's name, Enoch.

His descendants are numbered to the sixth generation. They gradually degenerated in their moral and spiritual condition till they became wholly corrupt before God. This corruption prevailed, and at length the Deluge was sent by God to prevent the final triumph of evil. Cain's name literally means, a possession; a spear. What does that tell us? Could it be a title for a tribe of anti-God rebels? Cain's hostile attitude towards God ran unchecked through his descendants and actually led to the flood. It was the major contributor for God to decide to destroy the earth.

It's interesting to see the lineage and the fruit of that lineage which was murder and open disobedience. As the story goes, Lamech killed someone and speaks about it to his family as if it were nothing.

The good thing is that all of Cain's family died in the flood. However, the sin of Cain continued beyond the flood into the new world. Why, you say? Because *"all have sinned and come short of the glory of God"* Romans 3:23 Paul tells us that Adam's sin brought death to the human race and it passed on to his descendants. Romans 5:12 A haughty and rebellious spirit was not limited to just Cain's family. His family was where it first appeared.

THE PATH OF THE RIGHTEOUS

Abel, Cain's brother was not angry with God. He learned the way to God and followed the path set before him. He was a tender of sheep, not a farmer. His name means: the noun לבה (*hebel*) means vapor, breath, or something very close to nothing. The famous saying "vanity of vanities; all is vanity" (Ecclesiastes 1:2) uses these words. (Abraim Publications Biblical Name Vault) However, he was the beginning of the righteous lineage mentioned in the Bible.

Jesus, speaking to the religious leaders of his day said this, "That upon you may come all the righteous blood shed upon the earth, from the blood of righteous Abel unto the blood of Zacharias son of Barachias, whom ye slew between the temple and the altar." Matthew 23:35 Plus, God accepted his offering which was in accord with what was expected.

Abel may have been a light weight but not in God's eyes. He showed respect and reverence to God, his Creator and sought to live in harmony with him. Nevertheless, there must have been a great deal of tension between Able and his brother Cain. Abel had a simple trust in God while Cain questioned God's wisdom and rejected his lead. This is obvious by his anger towards God when his offering was rejected.

Cain must have seen Abel as the favored one of the family. Why else would Cain turn his anger from God to Abel? Able didn't reject him, God did. But Cain took it out on Able. It's a clear case of misplaced hostility.

The story only says that Cain talked with his brother, Abel. It doesn't say what they talked about. I am guessing that it was Cain's rejection by God and how Cain felt about it. I am also guessing that Abel defended God, telling Cain all that he had to do is make his offering in accordance with God's instructions.

It certainly seems that Abel was killed by Cain because he did not support Cain's viewpoint. When they were in the field, as the story goes, Cain rose up and killed his brother, Abel. The anger he held for God was transferred to Abel and by striking out at Abel, Cain could also strike out at God. It was an act of revenge.

So, the first death on planet earth was by an act of cold-blooded murder and it was committed by the first person to be born of Adam & Eve.

THE SIGNIFICANCE OF THE STORY

Cain's Offering Is Rejected, Why?

Why was Cain's offering rejected by God? Pay attention now because it's very important to understand why. The entire Bible and salvation message is predicated on the answer.

We read in the story that the two brothers came to God with different offerings. Abel showed up before the Lord with a blood sacrifice whereas Cain offered the fruit of the ground, the results of his own labor.

You'll remember in Genesis, chapter one, that God cursed the ground and said it would not produce its full potential. He also said that man would work by the sweat of his brow. An offering that comes from the labor of man's hands and cursed by God could never be acceptable.

You will also remember that when Adam and Eve sinned, they could not cover their own shame. God had to slay an innocent animal and clothe them with its skin. This is the beginning of the blood sacrifice that would be required throughout the ages for the atonement for man's sin. Jewish history carried the practice on in an annual "Day of Atonement" ritual.

This practice of a blood sacrifice was a portrait of the ultimate sacrifice of the only begotten Son of God. They called his name Jesus. He was the anointed one (Christ) of God that pre-existed in heaven as God and was born of the virgin Mary and was the slain Lamb of God, before the foundation of the world. Hear what John Says in his gospel.

THE GOD-MAN

John 1:1-14 King James Version

"In the beginning was the Word, and the Word was with God, and the Word was God. The same was in the beginning with God. All things were made by Him, and without Him was not anything made that was made.

In Him was life, and that life was the Light of men. And the Light shineth in darkness, and the darkness comprehended it not. There was a man sent from God, whose name was John. The same came as a witness to bear witness of the Light, that all men through him might believe.

He was not that Light, but was sent to bear witness of that Light. That was the true Light which lighteth every man that cometh into the world. He was in the world, and the world was made by him, and the world knew him not.

He came unto His own, and his own received Him not. But as many as received him, to them gave the power to become the sons of God, even to those who believe in his name, who were born not of blood, nor of the will of the flesh, nor of the will of man, but of God.

And the Word was made flesh, and dwelt among us (and we beheld His glory, the glory as of the only Begotten of the Father), full of grace and truth."

So, here's what is being said; Jesus was the word in heaven. He was God and he was with God. All things were made by him. He is the Creator. He took upon himself human flesh, why?...to be the payment for sin so man could be forgiven and reinstated as the children of God.

1 John 2:2 - And he is the propitiation for our sins: and not for ours only, but also for the sins of the whole world. Jesus was the propitiation for sin as the Bible declares.

Propitiation is the biblical doctrine embodying the concept that the death of Christ fully satisfied the demands of a righteous God in respect to judgment upon the sinner.

Propitiation is one of the most important theological words that can help us understand what Jesus accomplished on the cross. It expresses the profound love and grace of both God the Father and Jesus Christ in providing a sacrifice that allows our sins to be forgiven so that we can receive the gift of salvation. Excerpts from Bibled.org

The concept of "Atonement" is focused on man and his cleansing from sin. The term Propitiation focuses on God who brings forth the sacrifice for the purpose of accomplishing justice and satisfying his own righteousness. They work hand and hand to produce the grace of God, through which man can be saved. Here-in is the beginning of a false teaching and the truth about salvation. The sacrifices are the beginnings of salvation by man's works and salvation by God's gift of Grace. Oddly enough, this battle between how man is redeemed has gone on down through the ages even unto this day.

Jesus taught that salvation was a free gift, given to whosoever believed in him. Listen to the famous Bible verse of John 3:16 where Jesus said, *"For God so loved the world, that he gave his only begotten Son, that whosoever believeth in him should not perish, but have everlasting life."*

We do the believing and God does the saving. It's that simple. He has made Jesus to become sin for us so we might be the righteousness of God in him. 11 Corinthians 5:21 There is no mention of, "Good Works" as a basis for one's salvation.

John 6:29 tells us, in the words of Jesus, "Jesus answered and said unto them, "This is the work of God, that ye believe on him whom he hath sent." …And what is it that we are to believe? It is that Jesus was God in human flesh, sent by God, the Father, to die for the sins of the entire human race.

When we believe in him, we trust in, rely upon and adhere to his teachings. We make him Lord over our lives and follow him as his disciple. We turn from our wicked ways, deny ourselves and seek to walk with him in his Spirit.

THE SEED OF THE WOMAN

Another reason we put our faith in Jesus is because he was and still is the seed of the woman. You'll remember that God, in his declaration of judgments, told the serpent that he would bruise the heel of the coming one but that coming one, who God called, "The Seed of the Woman" would crush his head. Hear what Genesis 3:115 says.

"And I will put enmity between thee and the woman, and between thy seed and her seed; it shall bruise thy head, and thou shalt bruise his heel."

The seed of the woman is a reference to a single individual, not many offspring. It is a reference to Jesus. Also, in human experience, there is no seed of a woman, only the seed of the man. Eve had no seed. This is a Biblical support text for the virgin birth. The seed came from God when the power of God overshadowed Mary and she conceived.

"And the angel answered and said unto her, The Holy Ghost shall come upon thee, and the power of the Highest shall overshadow thee: therefore, also that holy thing which shall be born of thee shall be called the Son of God." Luke 1:35-38

Had the seed been of Adam, it would carry with it a sinful DNA that would have made Jesus nothing more than a sinner like us. He would never qualify to be the spotless Lamb of God.

It's all about the offering. Cain rebelled and brought his own works to God that were produced from a ground that had been cursed by God and produced from the labor of his own efforts.

Abel followed God's directive, realizing that he could not redeem himself and he was indeed a sinner. He put his hopes in the coming one that God said would one day come and trusted in the blood sacrifice to cover his sin until that time came.

Some theologians say that the problem wasn't the offering but the attitude of Cain that cause his offering to be rejected. That is just not true because the foundation for salvation was and still is the blood sacrifice…the innocent for the guilty. This is the true gospel message and why our redemption cannot be earned. It's a free gift to all who believe.

There are many Christian churches today that teach salvation by works. They miss the heart of God and place their hope of salvation on their own effort. They never know if it is enough to satisfy God's acceptance. The fear of death looms over them and they are tormented by the devil that says, they didn't do enough or didn't work hard enough to qualify. We can know and rest in the love of God to save us. It's a matter of faith, not works. Salvation is of God, not man.

God's grace and his plan of salvation for the human race rests on the offering of Abel. Abel represents the beginning of the righteous lineage that would follow God in the earth. Cain killed Abel and destroyed the dream of God to place his image and likeness through mankind. However, God gave Eve another child, Seth, to replace Abel and continue his will.

THE SIN BEHIND THE SIN

The act of murder was indeed a sin against God and man. However, behind that sin lies another sin far worse. Cain didn't just kill his brother, Abel. He struck a deadly blow at the heart of God, destroying his eternal dream of manifesting his image and likeness on the earth.

Abel was the beginning of the righteous lineage through which the Messiah (Anointed One) would come. The sin behind the sin was to destroy the lineage before it had a chance to develop. This one act of murder, if allowed to stand, would keep the Messiah from being born and kill God's plan to not only redeem mankind but also to place his image on the earth.

It is obvious, to me anyway, that Satan had a hand in orchestrating this terrible event. His nature and image replaced the image and nature of God when Adan sinned. It was easy for Satan to motivate Cain. They thought alike and exhibited the same hostilities.

You'll remember that God told Adan that in the day you eat of the tree of the knowledge of good and evil, you shall surely die. Here's how it is worded in the King James Version… "But of the tree of the knowledge of good and evil, thou shalt not eat of it: for in the day that thou eat thereof thou shalt surely die." Genesis 2:17

Adam didn't die physically. He died spiritually. He found himself cut off from God. The "Breath of Life" that was breathed into him; that made him a living soul, was taken away. His Godly image and character became distorted, sinful and evil. It took on the nature and image of Satan.

Down the road in history, Ezekiel, the prophet would say, "The soul that sinneth, it shall die." Ezekiel 18:20 Also, Jeramiah, another prophet, would declare, "The heart is deceitful above all things, and desperately wicked: who can know it?" Jeremiah 17:9

Then in the New Testament, the apostle Paul would write to the church at Rome telling them,

"Wherefore, as by one man (That would be Adam) sin entered into the world, and death by sin; and so death passed upon all men, for that all have sinned." Romans 5:12

Mankind was now nothing more than walking dead men in servitude to Satan. That's why God sent his only begotten Son to save his precious creation and restore his image upon the earth. See John 3:16

Satan thought he had won the battle but he really underestimated God. God gave Eve a replacement that would carry on his Godly linage. See who it was in the Genesis account.

SIN LIETH AT THE DOOR

You'll remember that God told Cain that if he did well (the right thing) he would be accepted and if he did not, choosing to go against what God had set in place, sin would lie at his door. Genesis 4:7

That poetic phrase, "Sin Lieth At His Door", captures the nature of our rebellion against God. Sin desires to own us, and our refusal to let God set the standard for right and wrong. Cain didn't have to open the door to sin. He could have rejected the thought and submitted himself to the will of God. However, he did not. He opened the door and found it was the fast track to acting out the sin that now filled his heart.

THE CRY OF INNOCENT BLOOD

"And he (God) said, what hast thou done? the voice of thy brother's blood cries unto me from the ground." Genesis 4:10 Cain could not get away from the blood of his brother, Abel. Its voice cried out to God from the ground. His cry was for vengeance. Cain had to pay for his murderous act.

It's interesting to see that nothing gets past God. If we think no one is watching or that we can commit the perfect crime, we are sadly mistaken. Why? Because God sees all and knows all. In this case, the blood of Abel cried out from the ground for vengeance.

We must compare the innocent blood of Abel to the innocent blood of Jesus that flowed from the cross as he was being crucified. It places vengeance alongside mercy and shows God's forgiveness in a real way.

Here is what the writer of Hebrews says:

"But ye are come unto mount Sion, and unto the city of the living God, the heavenly Jerusalem, and to an innumerable company of angels, to the general assembly and church of the firstborn, which are written in heaven, and to God the Judge of all, and to the spirits of just men made perfect, and to Jesus the mediator of the new covenant, and to the blood of sprinkling, that speaks better things than that of Abel." Hebrews 12:22-24

The better things is a reference to mercy instead of vengeance. Jesus, himself even said, "No man taketh it (his life) from me, but I lay it down of myself. I have power to lay it down, and I have power to take it again. This commandment have I received of my Father." John 10:18

Jesus freely gave his life as the penalty for our sins. He was the blood sacrifice that was foreshadowed in the Old Testament by the blood sacrifice offered to God in the very beginning by Abel.

Here are a few other scriptures that reveal Jesus' willingness to lay down his own life for us:

John 10:11-I am the good shepherd. The good shepherd lays down his life for the sheep.

John 3:16-For God so loved the world, that he gave his only Son, that whoever believes in him should not perish but have eternal life.

I Peter 3:18-For Christ also suffered once for sins, the righteous for the unrighteous, that he might bring us to God, being put to death in the flesh but made alive in the spirit,

Ephesians 5:2-And walk in love, as Christ loved us and gave himself up for us, a fragrant offering and sacrifice to God

Romans 5:8-But God shows his love for us in that while we were still sinners, Christ died for us.

I Peter 2:24-He himself bore our sins in his body on the tree, that we might die to sin and live to righteousness. By his wounds you have been healed.

I John 2:2-He is the propitiation for our sins, and not for ours only but also for the sins of the whole world.

THE DIVINE REPLACEMENT

Seth, in Judaism and Christianity, was the third son of Adam and Eve and brother of Cain and Abel, their only other child mentioned by name in the Hebrew Bible. According to Genesis 4:25, Seth was born after Abel's murder by Cain, and Eve believed that God had appointed him as a replacement for Abel. (Bible Dictionary) Here's what she said,

"And Adam knew his wife again; and she bare a son, and called his name Seth: For God, said she, hath appointed me another seed instead of Abel, whom Cain slew. And to Seth, to him also there was born a son; and he called his name Enos: *then began men to call upon the name of the Lord.*" Genesis 4:25-26

God always accomplishes his will, no matter who or what gets in his way. The prophet Isiah said it well. "So shall my word be that goes forth out of my mouth: it shall not return unto me void, but it shall accomplish that which I please, and it shall prosper in the thing whereto I sent it." Isaiah 55:11

The greatest thing about serving the Lord is that he can do anything at any time. When all seems lost and there is no hope, God is still there and will move mountains to accomplish his will in your life. He is LORD over all the earth, the heavens and every creature.

THE SEED OF PROMISE

According to Genesis, Seth is the ancestor of Noah and hence the father of all mankind, all other humans having perished in the Great Flood. Late in life, Adam gave Seth secret teachings that would become the Kabbalah, although this is not confirmed. Seth is also considered the appointed offspring, the, "Seed of Promise", which ultimately would lead to the arrival of the Messiah. (Anointed On)

Seth was described as being of excellent character and virtuous. His descendants were wise and had a great knowledge of the heavenly bodies. They erected pillars, known as the "Sons of Seth," which were inscribed with science and were used to protect and remember Seth after he died. Based on Jewish reckoning, he was born in 130 AM. (Years after creation) According to Aggadah, he had 33 sons and 23 daughters. According to the Seder Olam Rabbah, he died in 1042 AM. Excerpts from Wikipedia.

CAIN, HIS CHILDREN & THEIR LEGACY

The sin behind the sin was a Satanic attach aimed at God and sent through Cain's evil heart. The 4th chapter of Genesis provides a list of Cain's descendants. We do not know if it is a full list or just a list of notables. In any event, we can surmise that Cain went on with his life and participated in the process of populating planet earth.

The Biblical account says that he went into the land of Nod which means the land of exile. It also refers to the land of wandering. Here's the record of Cain's descendants: (Genesis 4:17-24)

"And Cain knew his wife; and she conceived, and bare Enoch: and he built a city, and called the name of the city, after the name of his son, Enoch.

And unto Enoch was born Irad: and Irad begat Mehujael: and Mehujael begat Methusael: and Methusael begat Lamech. And Lamech took unto him two wives: the name of the one was Adah, and the name of the other Zillah.

And Adah bare Jabal: he was the father of such as dwell in tents, and of such as have cattle. And his brother's name was Jubal: he was the father of all such as handle the harp and organ. And Zillah, she also bare Tubalcain, an instructer of every artificer in brass and iron: and the sister of Tubalcain was Naamah.

And Lamech said unto his wives, Adah and Zillah, hear my voice; ye wives of Lamech, hearken unto my speech: for I have slain a man to my wounding, and a young man to my hurt. If Cain shall be avenged sevenfold, truly Lamech seventy and sevenfold."

THE ORIGIN OF POLYGAMY

Now we know where polygamy began. It was Lamech that went against the wishes of God. You'll remember God's statement when creating Eve. He said…

"And the LORD God said, *It is* not good that the man should be alone; I will make him an help meet for him." Genesis 2:18

If God wanted man to have more than one help meet, he would have provided them when he created woman. Instead, he made one woman for one man. What a concept.

ENOCH & ENOCH

After Cain arrived in the land of Nod, to which he was evicted by the Lord as his punishment for murdering his brother Abel, his wife became pregnant and bore Cain's first child, whom he named Enoch.

This Enoch is not to be confused with Enoch, son of Jared, to whom the authorship of the Book of Enoch is ascribed. The Book of Genesis says this Enoch lived 365 years before he was taken by God. The text reads that Enoch "walked with God: and he was no more; for God took him" (Genesis 5:21–24), which some Christians interpret as Enoch's entering Heaven alive. It is also believed that he will be one of the two witnesses spoken of in the book of Revelation that will return from heaven to witness against the Anti-Christ during the great tribulation. The other witness is Elijah, the prophet that was caught up in a fiery chariot into heaven.

Cain and/or Enoch built a city and named it after Enoch. However, this cannot be absolutely confirmed. There is a question as to who actually built the city, Cain or Enoch. We do know that the Cain family made tools of iron and brass and musical instruments. Enoch must have been a part of that.

THE DEATH OF CAIN & HOW HE DIED

Tradition tells us that Lamech killed Cain accidentally while on a hunting trip. He was a blind but skilled hunter. His son heard a noise and told Lamech where to shoot. Lamech shot off an arrow at the noise, thinking it was a wild animal. If you believe that, I have a bridge I want to sell you. We do not know how Cain died. I doubt it was at the hands of Lamech, his grandson.

Ancient books, like the book of Jubilees, suggest the theory that a house of stone fell on him and he died at **700** years old. Nevertheless, Cain was a wandered, isolated from his extended family and forced to wander from place to place. He could no longer till the ground because God said it would not yield for him.

THE MYSTERY OF CAIN'S WIFE

There has been much discussion over the centuries about Cain's wife. We are not given her name, only that Cain," Knew" her and she started to birth children. The question that lingers is, "Where did she come from?" Did she live in the land of Nod, the land of exile? Or did Cain marry her before he killed his brother and just took her along? Does it even matter? One theory says that Cain's wife was his sister.

The fact is, she chose to be or remain the wife of a killer and helped him to populate the earth with a lineage of rebellious anti-God offspring. It wasn't until Eve birthed Seth that men began to seek the Lord. Cain's lineage resulted in extreme wickedness that was present in Noah's day when God caused the flood to cleanse the earth from the influence of Cain's descendants.

Cain's descendants were builders, makers of Iron tools and musical instruments. They remained rebellious, vengeful and followed the character of Cain right up to the flood and the end of their world.

THE GENE POOL QUESTION

A gene pool is the collection of genes or alleles in an interbreeding population of a single species. It includes all the genetic information or material of the population at a given time. A gene pool can change over time through evolution[4] and affect the biological fitness and adaptability of the population.(Summarized from 5 sources and the web)

There are three types of human gene pools. The Primary Gene Pool is saying that the members in this pool are of the same species and can inter-mate freely. The peculiarity of this gene pool is that crossing is easy, producing fertile hybrids with good chromosome pairing, and normal gene segregation causing easy gene transfer.

This would have been the case with the origin of life and the birth of children that came from Adam

& Eve and other children down the line. Marrying within siblings or family would not affect the quality of life or genetic strength of the offspring. Thus, if Cain took his sister or a cousin as a wife, it would be ok.

THE MARK UPON CAIN

Much has been said about the mark of Cain. No one knows what that mark was. It was placed upon him, not as a curse by God, but as a protection to keep others from killing him. It came at the request of Cain, pleading to God for mercy. Some say it was the growth of a horn which supports the hunting accident, (looking like a wild animal) in tradition. Others say it was a letter placed on his face, visible to all that would meet him.

The mark of Cain was also used as a means to justify slavery in the 18th century. It was widely use as the reason for the existence of black or dark-skinned people. The slave traders said that they were considered inferior and substandard and the plantation owners who bought the slaves agreed so they could justify slave labor. This theory became the norm in society.

This, of course was ridiculous. If that were the case, not only Blacks but also Latino and almost 80% of the world population would be under the curse of Cain. Only 12% of the world population is considered Caucasian.

Hitler took this inferior race doctrine one step further and said that the Arian race was pure and the rest of the races were inferior. Coupled with Darwin's theory of evolution that replaced God, he justified the extermination of six million Jews and over 29 million people that disagreed with his views during WWII.

THE WAY OF CAIN

There is still one more Cain issue to discuss. That is the way of Cain. Cain was one of three Old Testament characters that errored in worship. The group consisted of three men who each had the particular error of trying to corrupt the rightful worship of God.

In the case of Cain, the implication is that God did not accept his sacrifice because he did not offer the correct sacrifice. He deviated from the blood sacrifice to the labor of his own hands. (Genesis 4:3-5)

The Stack Exchange tells us about the other two men.

In the case of Balaam, Numbers 34:16 says that he not only had intended to curse the Israelites, but that he had advised the Moabites into seducing the Israelites and getting them to worship Baal, which is told in Numbers 25.

In the case of Korah, Moses and Korah actually had a worship contest! (Numbers 16) Korah was a Levite, but he wasn't one of the priests, and so he wasn't allowed to do all that Aaron was. This made him jealous, but God confirmed that only those he said could present incense at the tabernacle.

We could add to the list Nadab and Abihu, Aaron's sons, who in Leviticus 10 burned "strange fire" at the tabernacle and were burned up by God. Creativity was a dangerous thing when it came to worshipping God at the tabernacle!

Jude 10 says that these people "do whatever their instincts tell them, and so they bring about their own destruction." We must be careful not to follow our instincts blindly, but check them against the revealed word of God.

GOD'S JUDGMENT OF CAIN

God judged Cain for his murderous act. Here's a list of punishments:

1. God exiled Cain from his presence. Their fellowship was over.
2. God marked Cain with a visible mark so others would not hurt him and would know to avoid him.
3. God cursed the ground so Cain, who was a farmer, could no longer practice his love for growing things.
4. A fugitive and a vagabond shalt thou be in the earth.
5. And now art thou cursed from the earth, which hath opened her mouth to receive thy brother's blood from thy hand.

Did Cain get away with murder? It doesn't look like it. God's judgment was really harsh and came swift upon Cain. Death would have been easier and a softer punishment. However, living out the punishment as a life sentence was worse than a swift death.

MODERN DAY LIFE APPLICATIONS

What can we learn from this story? We know it really happened because the Bible says so. Here-in is a list of things that can apply to our lives:

- Anger is not a good thing. We must not allow it to reside or take up residence in our hearts. If we do, we will be considered a fool. See Ecclesiastes 7:9
- The "Way of Cain" is to reject the blood sacrifice, replacing it with our own offering. This is against the will of God and puts us in an adversary relationship to God and subject to his judgment. We will be numbered with the wicked and cast into the lake of fire at the end of the world. Rejecting God's plan of salvation is rejecting him…not a good thing.

- Killing another person is destroying their dreams and it is listed in the 10-commandments as a "Thou Shalt Not." We must not take another's life or even destroy it with our angry words. Why? Because God will visit us with the same level of punishment so we know what it is to hurt inside. The Bible says Judge not, that you be not judged. For with the judgment, you pronounce you will be judged, and with the measure you use it will be measured to you. (Matthew 7:1-2)
- Character is defined as Good or Evil. There is no neutral ground or in-between. Jesus said, "You are either for me or against me." Matthew 12:30 and Luke 11:23 Cain was against God while Able was for God. The two lineages grew up together like wheat and tares. They are still intertwined even unto this day and will be until Jesus comes back. It behooves us to align our thoughts and actions with the good and blossom as a tree of righteousness before the Lord.
- Seeking the favor of God and his salvation by works is a slap in the face of God who offered it to all mankind as a free gift. The works of our own hands cannot save us from our own sin. We can only believe and receive his free gift.

- We can try to hide our shame as Adam & Eve did by covering it with fig leaves or like Cain did when he was asked by God, "Where is thy brother" and said, "Am I my brother's keeper." But our own efforts and our angry words can never hide our sin and shame. It will take the blood sacrifice of Jesus on the cross to cleanse us from sin. See I John 1:9

I am sure you'll see more life applications but these will get you started on thinking about them.

CONCLUSION

All of us, we humans, have been given a free will by God. We can choose the path in life that we so desire. We can walk the broad road that leads to destruction or we can walk the narrow road that leads to life eternal. See Jesus' teaching in Matthew 7:13-14.

Both Cain and Abel were of a fallen nature that was passed on from Adam. However,

Cain displayed a character of evil. It exemplified Jealousy, Murder, Hate, Anger and lots more. Galatians chapter five tells us the deeds of the flesh. They were all present in the Cain lineage.

Abel's lineage was one of submission to God and his will. His descendants followed God and enjoyed God's blessings. Both men chose the path and walked the road and lived out their beliefs, good or bad. We are doing the same. Let us therefor follow after righteousness and be a blessing to God and our fellow man.

ABOUT THE AUTHOR JOHN MARINELLI

John Marinelli is an independent author/publisher. He has authored several other books including: "Original Story Poems", "The Art of Writing Christian Poetry," "Pulpit Poems," "Moonlight & Mistletoe," "The Mysterious Stranger," "With Eagles Wings," "Mysteries & Miracles," "It Came To Pass," Why Do The Righteous Suffer," "Believer's Handbook of Battle Strategies.", "Hidden In Plain Sight", "Heaven, Hell & Beyond", "The Life & Destiny of The God-Man", "The Return of Jesus Christ to

Planet Earth", How to Be Happy", "How to Live A Victorious Christian Life', "Morning Reign" and several more.

John is an accomplished Christian poet. He also dabbles in songwriting and writing children's books. John is a strong believer in the Bible and a minister of the gospel. He is retired and lives with his wife in north central Florida where he sings karaoke, plays chess, and write poedtry under the inspiration of the Holy Spirit.

Other books by John Marinelli can be viewed and purchased at: www.marinellichristianbooks.com

www.ingramcontent.com/pod-product-compliance
Lightning Source LLC
Chambersburg PA
CBHW020431010526
44118CB00010B/520